CSS Grid Layout

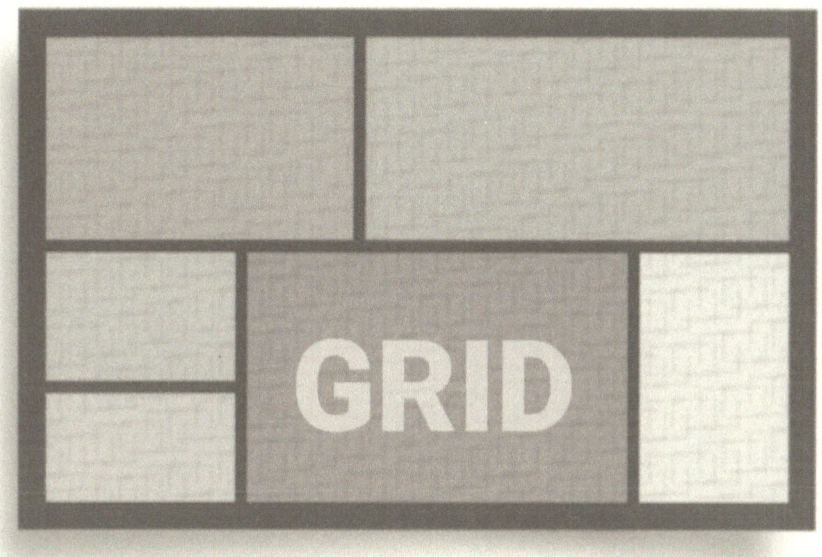

Abdelfattah Ragab

CSS Grid Layout

Abdelfattah Ragab

Introduction

Welcome to "CSS Grid Layout". In this book you will learn all about the CSS grid layout model and how to create complex and responsive grid-based designs. You will learn about all the properties of grid containers and grid elements.

By the end of this book, you will be able to use the grid layout to create responsive layouts and handle all kinds of scenarios.

Let's get started.

key concepts

CSS3 Grid Layout is a powerful two-dimensional layout system that allows you to create complex grid-based layouts on web pages. It provides precise control over the placement and alignment of elements within a grid container. Here's an overview of CSS3 Grid Layout and its key concepts:

Grid Container

- To create a grid layout, you need to designate an element as the grid container by applying the display: grid property.
- The grid container can be either a block-level or inline-level element.

Grid Tracks and Grid Cells

- Grid tracks are the columns and rows that make up the grid layout.
- By default, tracks are created automatically based on the content and size of the grid items.

- You can also explicitly define tracks using properties like grid-template-columns and grid-template-rows.

Grid Items

- Grid items are the elements placed inside the grid container.
- They can occupy one or more grid cells, spanning across multiple rows and columns.
- Use the grid-column and grid-row properties to position and span grid items within the grid.

Grid Lines

- Grid lines are the horizontal and vertical lines that define the boundaries of the grid cells and tracks.
- They can be referred to using line numbers or names assigned to them.

Grid Areas

- Grid areas are rectangular areas formed by combining multiple grid cells.

- You can assign names to grid areas using the grid-template-areas property.
- By referencing these area names, you can easily position grid items within specific areas.

Grid Template

- The grid template is used to define the structure of the grid by specifying the size and arrangement of tracks.
- Use properties like grid-template-columns, grid-template-rows, and grid-template-areas to create the grid template.

Grid Gap

- Grid gap refers to the spacing between grid cells and tracks.
- Use properties like grid-column-gap and grid-row-gap to define the size of the gap.
- grid-gap is a shorthand property that sets both column and row gaps simultaneously.

Alignment and Justification

- CSS Grid provides various properties to control the alignment and justification of grid items.
- Use properties like justify-items, align-items, justify-content, and align-content to align items within the grid container.
- Additionally, justify-self and align-self properties can be used to override alignment for individual grid items.

CSS3 Grid Layout offers a robust and flexible way to create complex layouts. By combining grid-related properties and techniques, you can achieve responsive and dynamic grid-based designs for your web pages. Experimenting with these properties and their combinations will help you harness the full potential of CSS3 Grid Layout.

The CSS grid Layout is a two-dimensional layout that allows you to design the layout with rows and columns. To create a grid layout, you need to designate an element as the grid container by applying the display: grid property.

```
.wrapper {
  display: grid;
}
```

Grid tracks are the columns and rows that make up the grid layout.

By default, tracks are created automatically based on the content and size of the grid items.

You can also explicitly define tracks using properties like grid-template-columns and grid-template-rows.

We have an example with some div elements like this

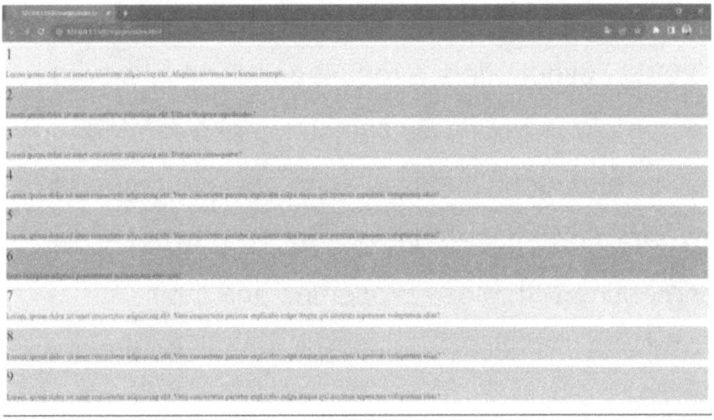

The space around the elements is set by the browser by default, and you can remove it by using the universal selector as follows

```
* {
  margin: 0;
  padding: 0;
}
```

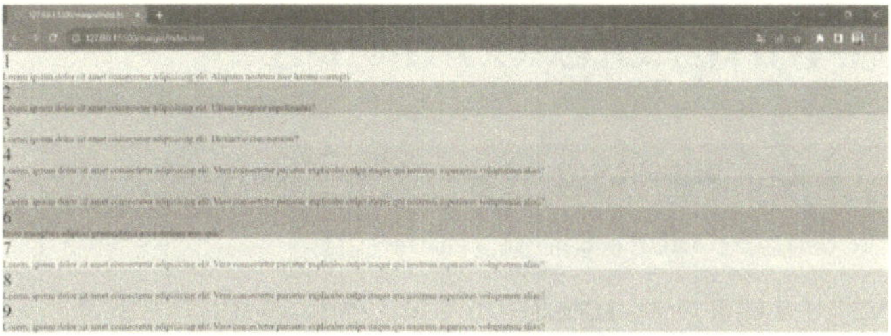

To make this a grid layout, I will set display: grid; to the container,

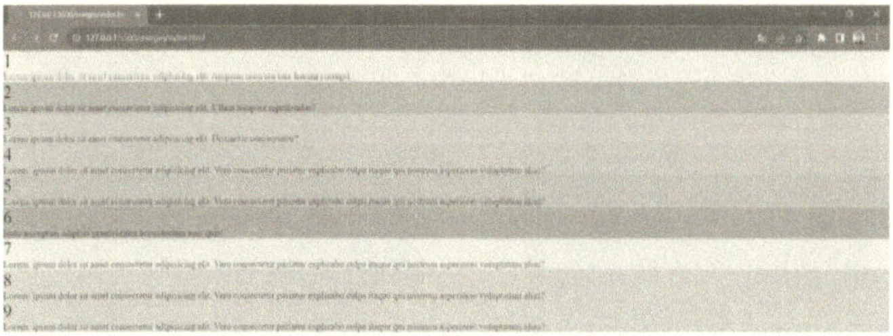

Now it is a grid layout, but it has no columns defined.

```css
.wrapper {
    display: grid;
}
```

Now it is a grid layout, but it has no columns defined.

grid-template-columns

The grid-template-columns property defines the number (and width) of columns in a grid layout.

The values are a space-separated list in which each value specifies the size of the respective column.

Values

- none
- auto
- max-content
- min-content
- length

none

Default value. Columns are created if needed

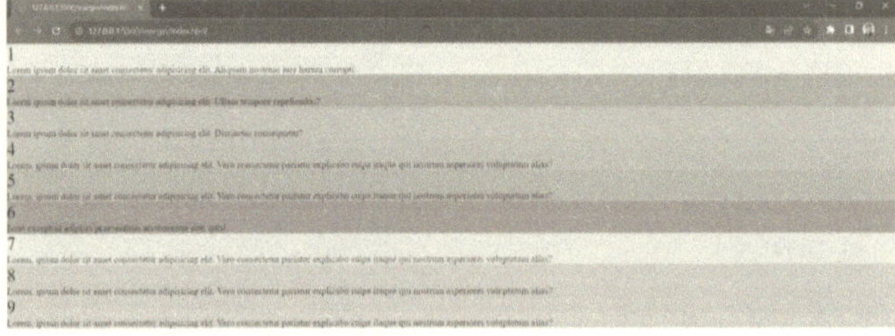

```css
<style>
  * {
    margin: 0;
    padding: 0;
  }
  .wrapper {
    display: grid;
    grid-template-columns: none;
  }
  .wrapper div span {
    font-size: 30px;
  }
  .div-1 {
    background-color: aqua;
  }
  .div-2 {
    background-color: cornflowerblue;
  }
  .div-3 {
    background-color: limegreen;
  }
  .div-4 {
    background-color: darkorange;
  }
  .div-5 {
    background-color: hotpink;
```

```css
  }
  .div-6 {
    background-color: mediumorchid;
  }
  .div-7 {
    background-color: springgreen;
  }
  .div-8 {
    background-color: lightsalmon;
  }
  .div-9 {
    background-color: darkturquoise;
  }
</style>
<div class="wrapper">
  <div class="div-1">
    <span>1</span>
    <p>
      Lorem ipsum dolor sit amet consectetur
adipisicing elit. Aliquam nostrum
      iure harum corrupti.
    </p>
  </div>
  <div class="div-2">
    <span>2</span>
    <p>
```

```html
      Lorem ipsum dolor sit amet consectetur
adipisicing elit. Ullam tempore
      repellendus?
    </p>
  </div>
  <div class="div-3">
    <span>3</span>
    <p>
      Lorem ipsum dolor sit amet consectetur
adipisicing elit. Distinctio
      consequatur?
    </p>
  </div>
  <div class="div-4">
    <span>4</span>
    <p>
      Lorem, ipsum dolor sit amet consectetur
adipisicing elit. Vero consectetur
      pariatur explicabo culpa itaque qui
nostrum asperiores voluptatum alias?
    </p>
  </div>
  <div class="div-5">
    <span>5</span>
    <p>
```

```
      Lorem, ipsum dolor sit amet consectetur
adipisicing elit. Vero consectetur
      pariatur explicabo culpa itaque qui
nostrum asperiores voluptatum alias?
    </p>
  </div>
  <div class="div-6">
    <span>6</span>
    <p>Iusto excepturi adipisci praesentium
accusantium eius quis!</p>
  </div>
  <div class="div-7">
    <span>7</span>
    <p>
      Lorem, ipsum dolor sit amet consectetur
adipisicing elit. Vero consectetur
      pariatur explicabo culpa itaque qui
nostrum asperiores voluptatum alias?
    </p>
  </div>
  <div class="div-8">
    <span>8</span>
    <p>
      Lorem, ipsum dolor sit amet consectetur
adipisicing elit. Vero consectetur
```

```
        pariatur explicabo culpa itaque qui
nostrum asperiores voluptatum alias?
    </p>
  </div>
  <div class="div-9">
    <span>9</span>
    <p>
        Lorem, ipsum dolor sit amet consectetur
adipisicing elit. Vero consectetur
        pariatur explicabo culpa itaque qui
nostrum asperiores voluptatum alias?
    </p>
  </div>
</div>
```

auto

The size of the columns depends on the size of the container and the size of the content of the articles in the column

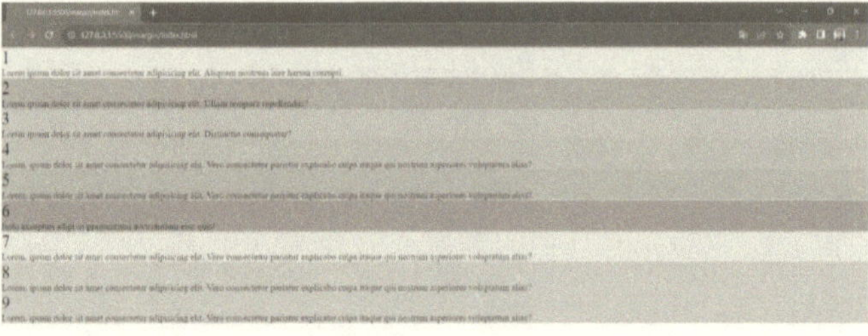

```css
.wrapper {
  display: grid;
  grid-template-columns: auto;
}
```

max-content

Sets the size of each column to depend on the largest item in the column

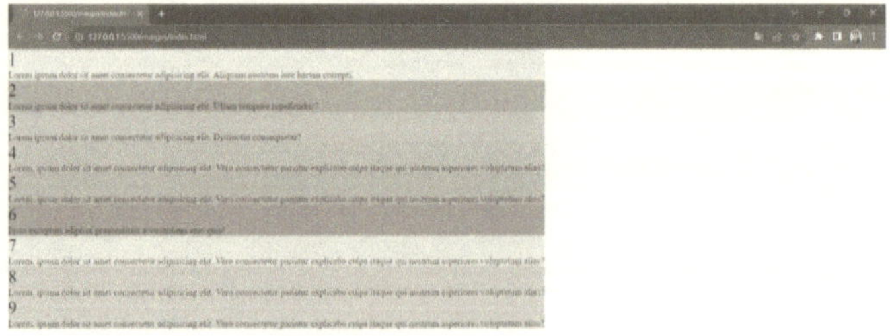

```css
.wrapper {
  display: grid;
  grid-template-columns: max-content;
}
```

min-content

Sets the size of each column to depend on the smallest
item in the column

```css
.wrapper {
  display: grid;
  grid-template-columns: min-content;
}
```

length

Sets the size of the columns, by using a legal length
value.

Set fixed width to the second column, 300px;

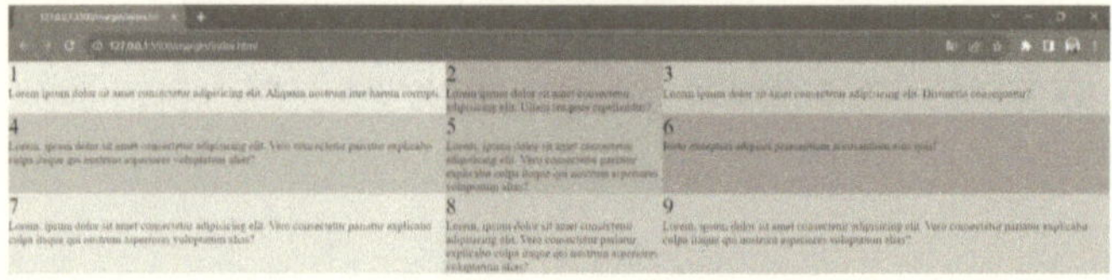

```css
.wrapper {
  display: grid;
  grid-template-columns: auto 300px auto;
}
```

%

Set the third column to be 50% of the container width:

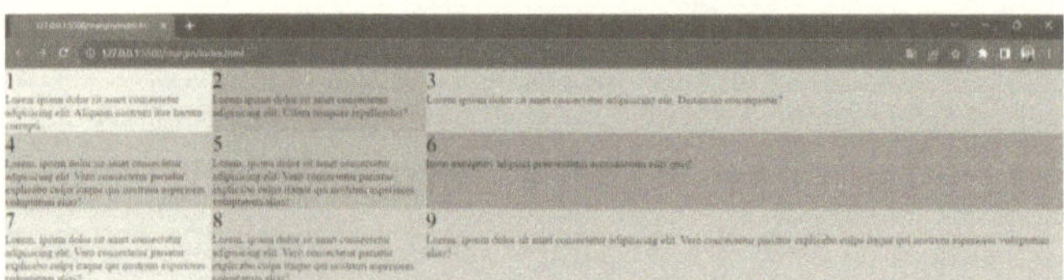

```css
.wrapper {
   display: grid;
   grid-template-columns: auto auto 60%;
}
```

fr

The `fr` unit represents a fraction of the available space
in the grid container.

Set the the third column to be 3 times larger than the
second column, while giving the first column fixed
500px:

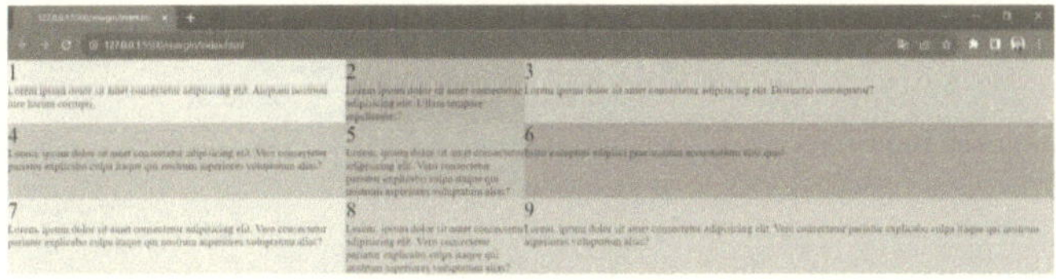

```css
.wrapper {
   display: grid;
   grid-template-columns: 500px 1fr 3fr;
}
```

minmax()

The CSS function minmax() defines a size range that is greater than or equal to min and less than or equal to max.

Set the second column has minimum 500px and maximum 2fr;

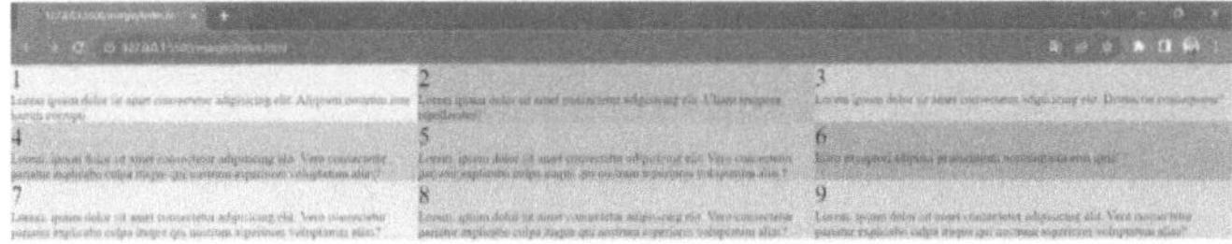

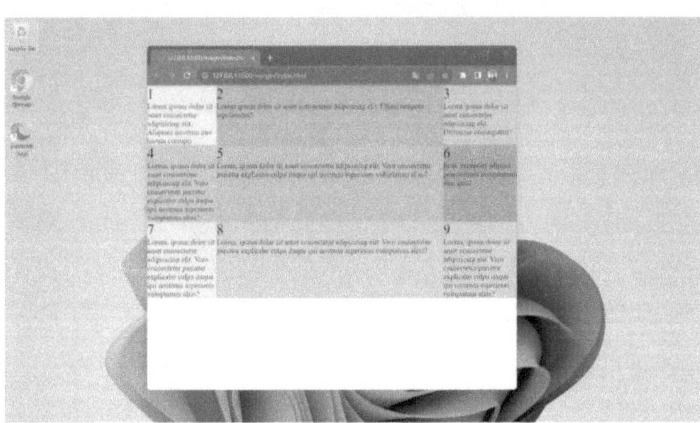

```
.wrapper {
```

```css
    display: grid;

    grid-template-columns: auto minmax(500px,
2fr) auto;
  }
```

repeat()

The CSS function repeat() represents a repeating fragment of the track list and makes it possible to write a large number of columns or rows that have a recurring pattern in a more compact form.

I want to have five columns and four of them will have the same width

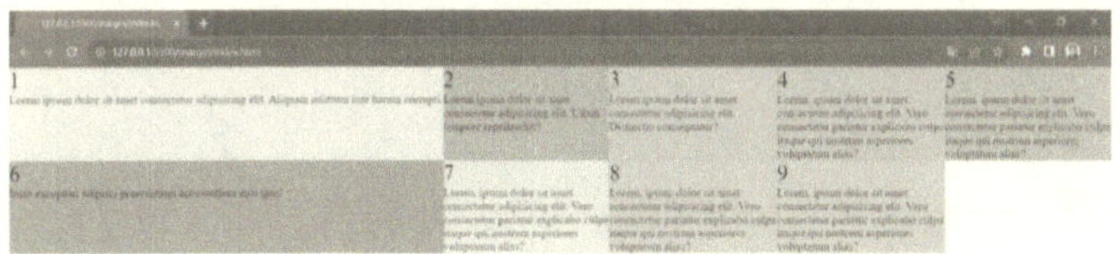

```css
  .wrapper {
    display: grid;
```

```css
    grid-template-columns: auto 1fr 1fr 1fr
1fr;
}
```

You can use the repeat() function for such scenarios as follows

```css
.wrapper {
  display: grid;
  grid-template-columns: auto repeat(4,
1fr);
}
```

auto, repeat() and length

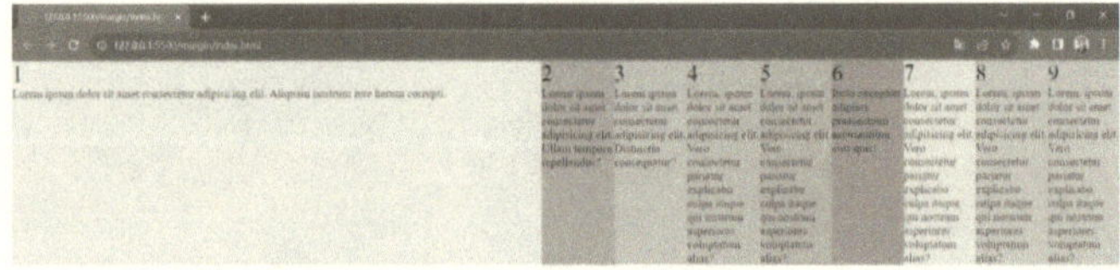

```css
.wrapper {
  display: grid;
```

```
grid-template-columns: auto repeat(8,
100px);
    }
```

grid-template-rows

The grid-template-rows property defines the number (and height) of rows in a grid layout.

The values are a space-separated list in which each value specifies the height of the respective row.

Values

- none
- auto
- max-content
- min-content
- length

none

No size is set. Rows are created if needed

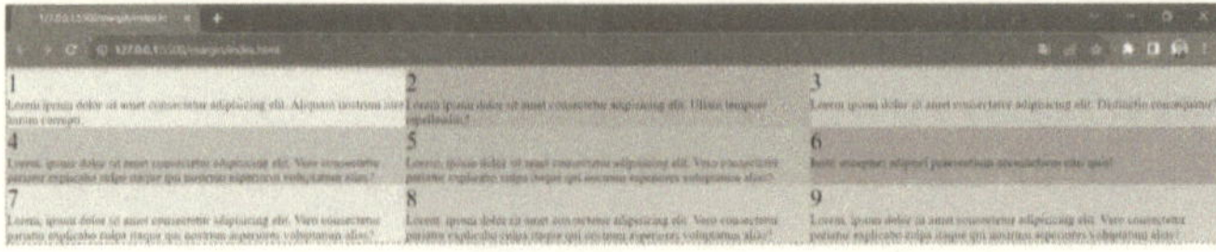

```css
.wrapper {
  display: grid;
  grid-template-columns: auto auto auto;
  border: 3px dashed orangered;
  grid-template-rows: none;
}
```

auto

The size of the rows is determined by the size of the container, and on the size of the content of the items in the row

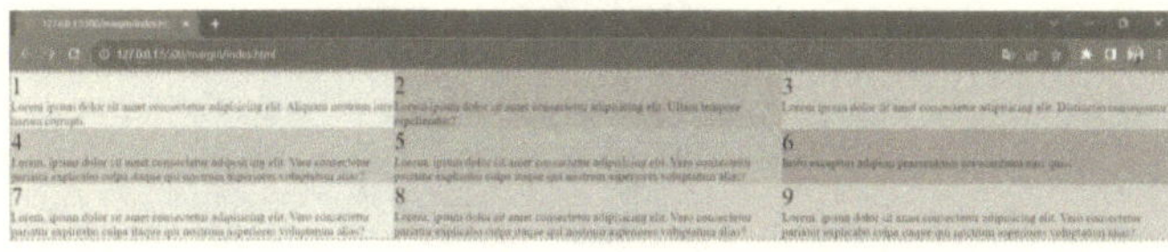

```css
.wrapper {
  display: grid;
  grid-template-columns: auto auto auto;
  border: 3px dashed orangered;
  grid-template-rows: auto;
}
```

max-content

Sets the size of each row to depend on the largest item in the row

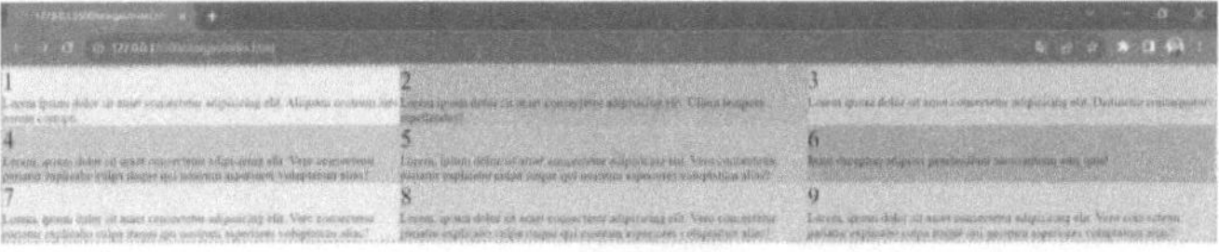

```css
.wrapper {
  display: grid;
  grid-template-columns: auto auto auto;
  border: 3px dashed orangered;
  grid-template-rows: max-content;
}
```

min-content

Sets the size of each row to depend on the smallest item in the row.

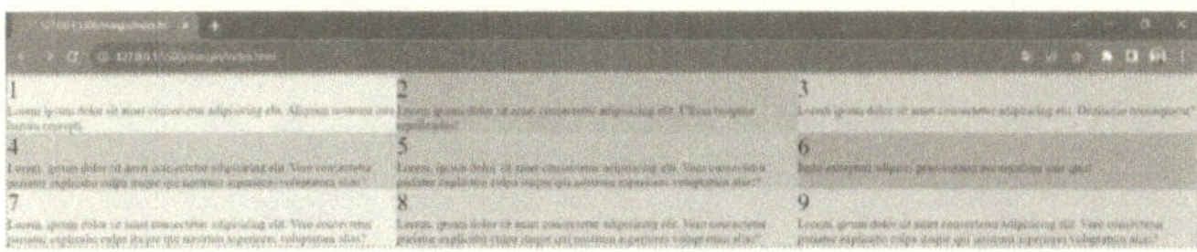

```css
.wrapper {
  display: grid;
  grid-template-columns: auto auto auto;
  border: 3px dashed orangered;
  grid-template-rows: min-content;
}
```

length

Sets the size of the rows, by using a legal length value.
Now we define four rows for the grid, each with a height
of 150px:

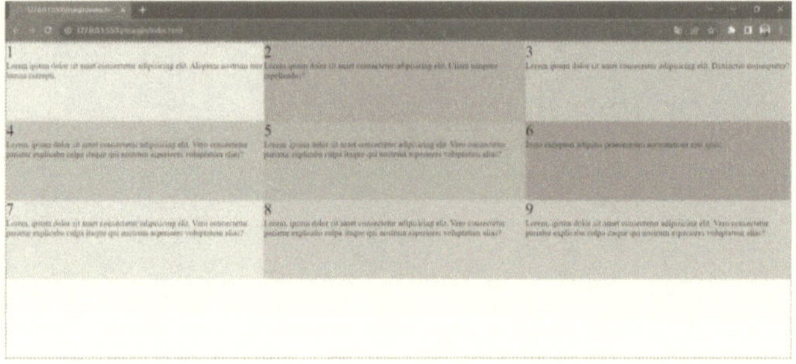

```
.wrapper {
  display: grid;
  border: 3px dashed orangered;
  grid-template-columns: auto auto auto;
  grid-template-rows: repeat(4, 150px);
}
```

So far we have worked with the grid container and the grid tracks, now we want to talk about the grid elements. By this I mean the elements that are placed within the grid container.

Grid items can occupy one or more grid cells, spanning across multiple rows and columns.

Use the grid-column and grid-row properties to position and span the elements within the grid.

Grid lines

First you need to know about grid lines.

Grid lines are created when you define tracks in the CSS Grid Layout.

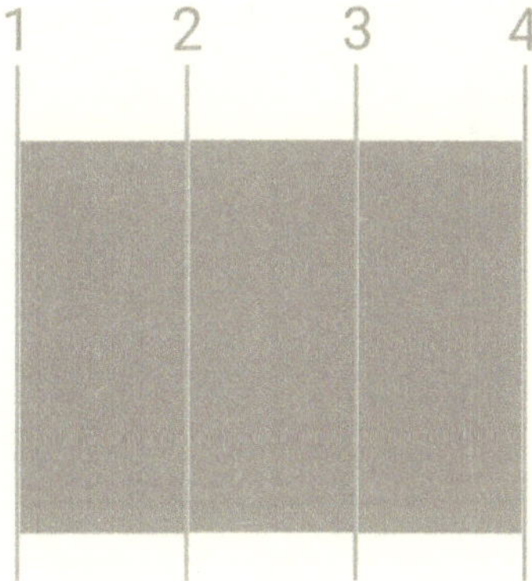

Here are the grid lines for a 3-column layout.

The same applies to the rows.

We use grid lines to determine the start and end for each grid element.

grid-column

The grid-column property defines the size and position of a grid element in a grid layout and is a short form for the grid-column-start and grid-column-end properties.

Values

- <grid-column-start> / <grid-column-end>

Values for grid-column-start and grid-column-end

- auto
- span n
- column-line

auto

Default value. The item will be placed following the flow

span n

Specifies the number of columns the item will span

Specifies in which column the display of the element should begin or end

grid-row

The grid-row property defines the size and position of a grid element in a grid layout and is a short form for the grid-row-start and grid-row-end properties

Values

- <grid-row-start> / <grid-row-end>

Values for grid-row-start and grid-row-end

- auto
- span n
- column-line

Default value. The item will be placed following the flow

Specifies the number of rows the item will span

row-line

Specifies in which row the display of the element should begin or end

auto

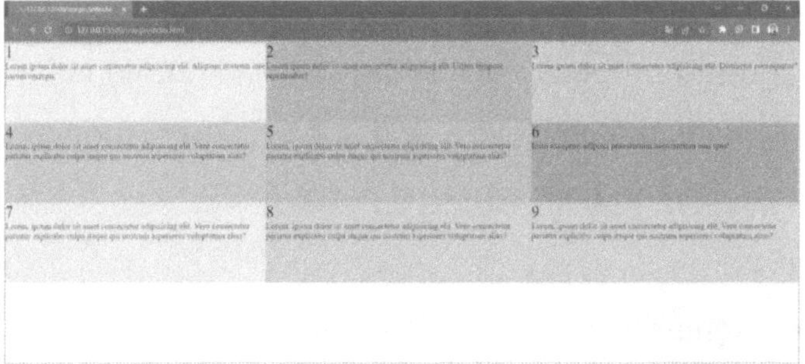

```css
.div-1 {
  background-color: aqua;
  grid-column: auto;
  grid-row: auto;
}
```

span n

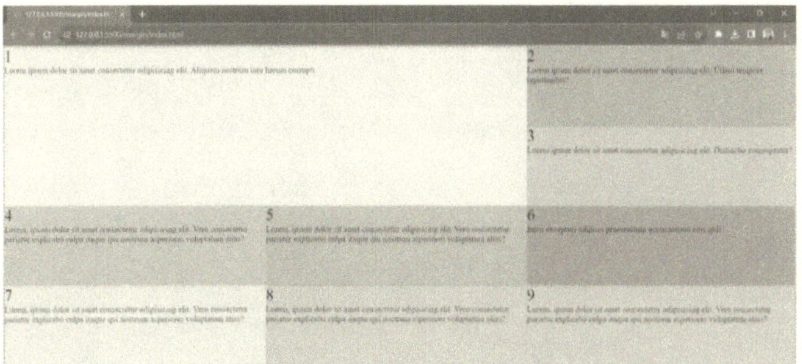

```css
.div-1 {
  background-color: aqua;
  grid-column: 1 / span 2;
  grid-row: 1 / span 2;
}
```

column-line and row-line

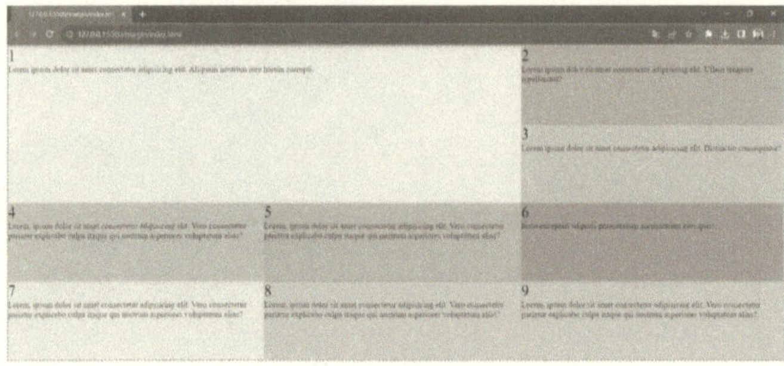

```css
.div-1 {
    background-color: aqua;
    grid-column: 1 / 3;
    grid-row: 1 / 3;
}
```

For the column, I specify that it begins in line 1 and ends in line 3.

I do the same for the row, I set it so that it starts in line 1 and ends in line 3.

So you can write the code like this and it will give the same result

```css
.div-1 {
    background-color: aqua;
    grid-column-start: 1;
    grid-column-end: 3;
```

```css
    grid-row-start: 1;
    grid-row-end: 3;
}
```

For the sake of simplicity, I use the shorthand property.

```css
.div-1 {
    background-color: aqua;
    grid-column: 1 / 3;
    grid-row: 1 / 3;
}
```

negative lines

If a negative integer is specified, it is counted backwards instead, starting with the end edge of the explicit grid. For example, I can span all columns by setting start to 1 and end to -1, as follows

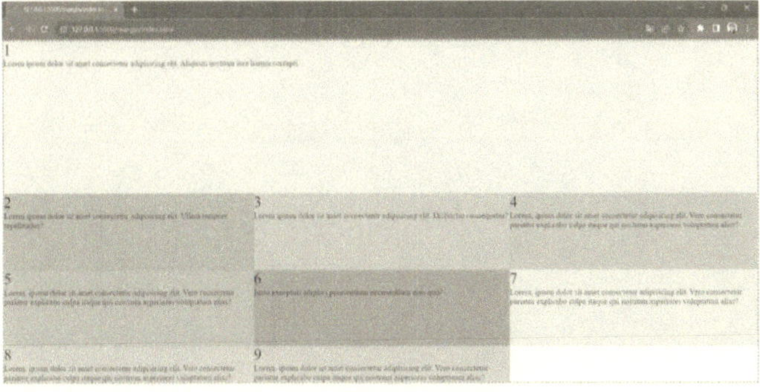

```css
.div-1 {
  background-color: aqua;
  grid-column: 1 / -1;
  grid-row: 1 / 3;
}
```

backwards

Negatives are counted backwards, starting with the end edge of the explicit grid.

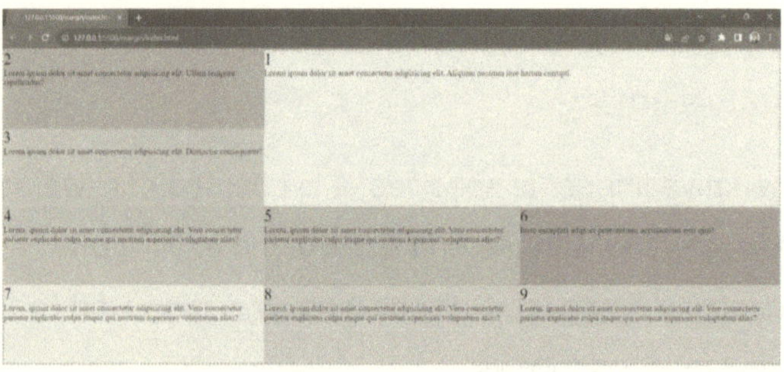

```css
.div-1 {
  background-color: aqua;
  grid-column: -1 / -3;
  grid-row: 1 / 3;
}
```

grid-template-areas

The grid-template-areas property defines areas within the grid layout.

Each area is defined by apostrophes. Use a dot character to refer to a grid element without a name.

Values

- none
- areas

none

Default value. No named grid areas

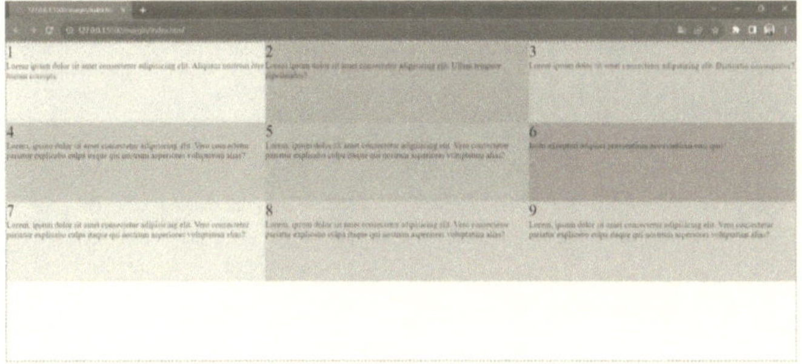

```
.wrapper {
  display: grid;
  border: 3px dashed orangered;
```

```css
    grid-template-columns: auto auto auto;
    grid-template-rows: repeat(4, 150px);
    grid-template-areas: none;
}
```

areas

A sequence that specifies how each columns and row should display

Each area is defined by apostrophes.

Use a dot character to refer to a grid element without a name.

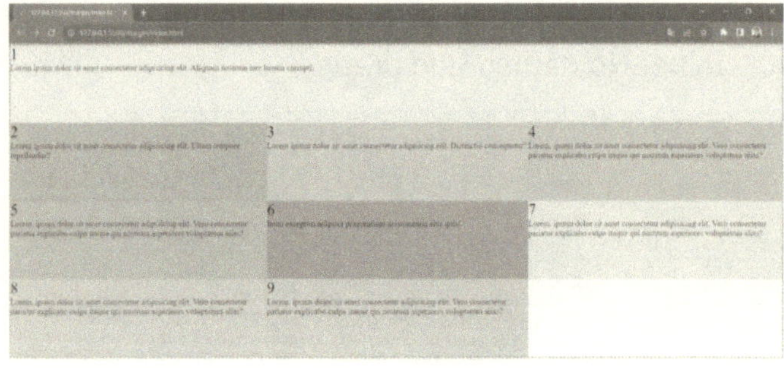

```css
.wrapper {
    display: grid;
    grid-template-columns: auto auto auto;
    grid-template-rows: repeat(4, 150px);
    border: 3px dashed orangered;
```

```css
    grid-template-areas:
        "a a a"
        ". . ."
        ". . .";
}
```

For the children elements, I want the .div-1 element to display in the "a" area.

```css
.div-1 {
    background-color: aqua;
    grid-area: a;
}
```

Here's the complete code:

```html
<style>
    * {
        margin: 0;
        padding: 0;
    }
    .wrapper {
        display: grid;
        grid-template-columns: auto auto auto;
        grid-template-rows: repeat(4, 150px);
        border: 3px dashed orangered;
        grid-template-areas:
            "a a a"
            "b c c"
```

```css
    "b c c";
}
.wrapper div span {
  font-size: 30px;
}
.div-1 {
  background-color: aqua;
  grid-area: a;
}
.div-2 {
  background-color: cornflowerblue;
}
.div-3 {
  background-color: limegreen;
}
.div-4 {
  background-color: darkorange;
}
.div-5 {
  background-color: hotpink;
}
.div-6 {
  background-color: mediumorchid;
}
.div-7 {
  background-color: springgreen;
```

```html
    }
    .div-8 {
      background-color: lightsalmon;
    }
    .div-9 {
      background-color: darkturquoise;
    }
</style>
<div class="wrapper">
  <div class="div-1">
    <span>1</span>
    <p>
      Lorem ipsum dolor sit amet consectetur
adipisicing elit. Aliquam nostrum
      iure harum corrupti.
    </p>
  </div>
  <div class="div-2">
    <span>2</span>
    <p>
      Lorem ipsum dolor sit amet consectetur
adipisicing elit. Ullam tempore
      repellendus?
    </p>
  </div>
  <div class="div-3">
```

```html
    <span>3</span>
    <p>
      Lorem ipsum dolor sit amet consectetur
  adipisicing elit. Distinctio
      consequatur?
    </p>
  </div>
  <div class="div-4">
    <span>4</span>
    <p>
      Lorem, ipsum dolor sit amet consectetur
  adipisicing elit. Vero consectetur
      pariatur explicabo culpa itaque qui
  nostrum asperiores voluptatum alias?
    </p>
  </div>
  <div class="div-5">
    <span>5</span>
    <p>
      Lorem, ipsum dolor sit amet consectetur
  adipisicing elit. Vero consectetur
      pariatur explicabo culpa itaque qui
  nostrum asperiores voluptatum alias?
    </p>
  </div>
  <div class="div-6">
```

```
<span>6</span>
<p>Iusto excepturi adipisci praesentium
accusantium eius quis!</p>
</div>
<div class="div-7">
<span>7</span>
<p>
Lorem, ipsum dolor sit amet consectetur
adipisicing elit. Vero consectetur
pariatur explicabo culpa itaque qui
nostrum asperiores voluptatum alias?
</p>
</div>
<div class="div-8">
<span>8</span>
<p>
Lorem, ipsum dolor sit amet consectetur
adipisicing elit. Vero consectetur
pariatur explicabo culpa itaque qui
nostrum asperiores voluptatum alias?
</p>
</div>
<div class="div-9">
<span>9</span>
<p>
```

```
        Lorem, ipsum dolor sit amet consectetur
adipisicing elit. Vero consectetur
        pariatur explicabo culpa itaque qui
nostrum asperiores voluptatum alias?
    </p>
  </div>
</div>
```

You can give it meaningful names like "head", "nav", "main" … etc.

```
  .wrapper {
    display: grid;
    grid-template-columns: auto auto auto;
    grid-template-rows: repeat(4, 150px);
    border: 3px dashed orangered;
    grid-template-areas:
      "head head head"
      "nav main main"
      "nav main main";
  }
```

gap

grid-gap is obsolete and is replaced by **gap**

The gap property defines the size of the gap between the rows and columns in a grid layout, and is a shorthand property for the following properties: row-gap and column-gap.

Values

- <row-gap> <column-gap>

gap: 20px;

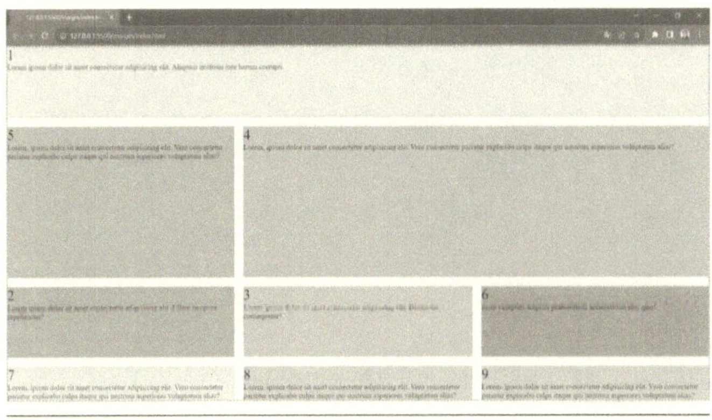

```css
.wrapper {
    display: grid;
    grid-template-columns: auto auto auto;
    grid-template-rows: repeat(4, 150px);
    border: 3px dashed orangered;
    grid-template-areas:
        "a a a"
        ". . ."
        ". . .";
    gap: 20px;
```

}

gap: 50px 10px;

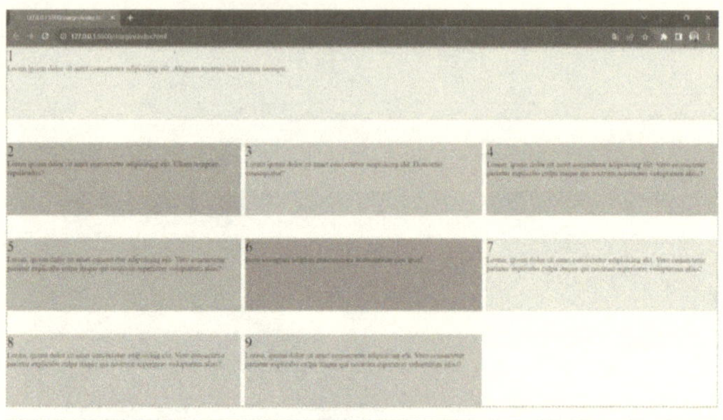

```css
.wrapper {
    display: grid;
    grid-template-columns: auto auto auto;
    grid-template-rows: repeat(4, 150px);
    border: 3px dashed orangered;
    grid-template-areas:
        "a a a"
        ". . ."
        ". . .";
    gap: 50px 10px;
}
```

column-gap: 20px;

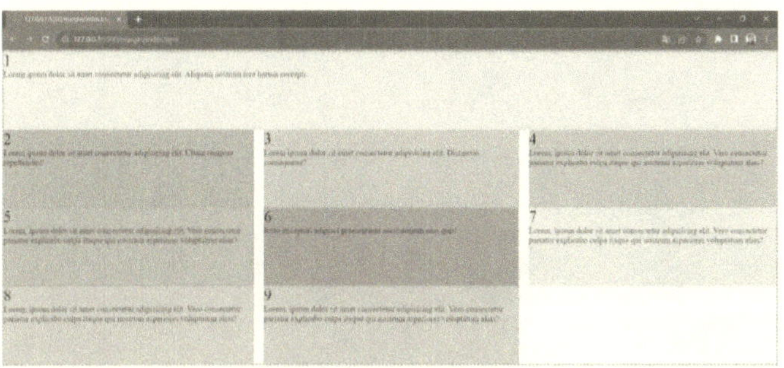

```css
.wrapper {
  display: grid;
  grid-template-columns: auto auto auto;
  grid-template-rows: repeat(4, 150px);
  border: 3px dashed orangered;
  grid-template-areas:
    "a a a"
    ". . ."
    ". . .";
  column-gap: 20px;
}
```

row-gap: 20px;

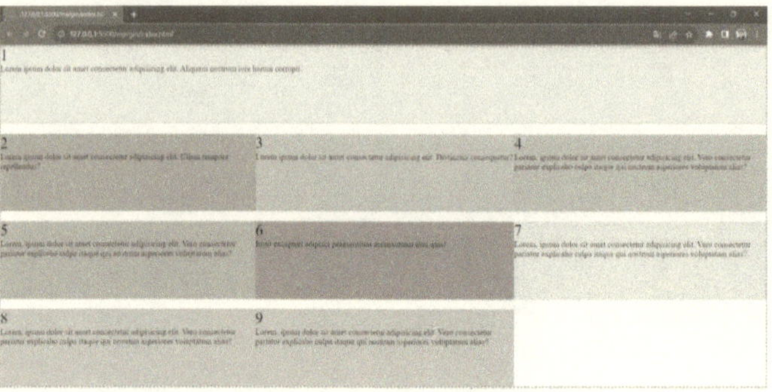

```css
.wrapper {
  display: grid;
  grid-template-columns: auto auto auto;
  grid-template-rows: repeat(4, 150px);
  border: 3px dashed orangered;
  grid-template-areas:
    "a a a"
    ". . ."
    ". . .";
  row-gap: 20px;
}
```

Alignment and Justification

CSS Grid Layout is a two-dimensional layout method that makes it possible to arrange content in rows and columns. Therefore, there are two axes in each grid. The block or column axis and the inline or row axis.

Inline Axis

The inline axis is the axis that corresponds to the direction in which the words in a sentence would run in the spelling used. In a horizontal language such as English or Arabic, the inline direction is therefore horizontal. In a vertical writing mode, the inline axis is vertical.

To align things on the inline axis, use the properties that start with justify-, justify-content, justify-items and justify-self.

Block axis

The block axis crosses the inline axis in the direction in which the blocks are displayed on the page — for example, paragraphs are displayed vertically one below the other in English. This is therefore the block dimension.

To align things to the block axis, use the properties that start with align-, align-content, align-items and align-self.

justify-content

The CSS property justify-content determines how the browser distributes the space between and around content elements along the inline axis of a grid container.

Values

- start or flex-start
- end or flex-end
- center
- space-between
- space-around
- space-evenly

start or flex-start

Default value. Items are positioned at the beginning of the container

`flex-start` is specific to flex layout, but if you use it with grid layout, it will be treated as `start`.

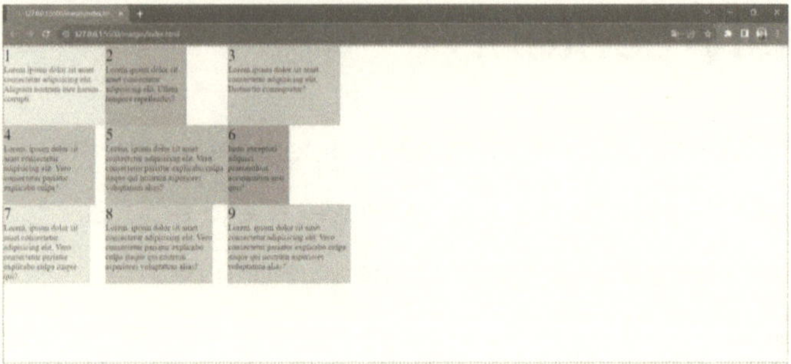

```css
<style>
  * {
    margin: 0;
    padding: 0;
  }
  .wrapper {
    display: grid;
    grid-template-columns: auto auto auto;
    grid-template-rows: repeat(4, 150px);
    border: 3px dashed orangered;
    justify-content: start;
  }
  .wrapper div span {
    font-size: 30px;
  }
  .div-1 {
    background-color: aqua;
```

```css
  width: 200px;
}
.div-2 {
  background-color: cornflowerblue;
  width: 160px;
}
.div-3 {
  background-color: limegreen;
  width: 220px;
}
.div-4 {
  background-color: darkorange;
  width: 180px;
}
.div-5 {
  background-color: hotpink;
  width: 240px;
}
.div-6 {
  background-color: mediumorchid;
  width: 120px;
}
.div-7 {
  background-color: springgreen;
  width: 170px;
}
```

```css
  .div-8 {
    background-color: lightsalmon;
    width: 210px;
  }
  .div-9 {
    background-color: darkturquoise;
    width: 240px;
  }
</style>
<div class="wrapper">
  <div class="div-1">
    <span>1</span>
    <p>
      Lorem ipsum dolor sit amet consectetur
adipisicing elit. Aliquam nostrum
      iure harum corrupti.
    </p>
  </div>
  <div class="div-2">
    <span>2</span>
    <p>
      Lorem ipsum dolor sit amet consectetur
adipisicing elit. Ullam tempore
      repellendus?
    </p>
  </div>
```

```html
<div class="div-3">
  <span>3</span>
  <p>
    Lorem ipsum dolor sit amet consectetur
adipisicing elit. Distinctio
    consequatur?
  </p>
</div>
<div class="div-4">
  <span>4</span>
  <p>
    Lorem, ipsum dolor sit amet consectetur
adipisicing elit. Vero consectetur
    pariatur explicabo culpa?
  </p>
</div>
<div class="div-5">
  <span>5</span>
  <p>
    Lorem, ipsum dolor sit amet consectetur
adipisicing elit. Vero consectetur
    pariatur explicabo culpa itaque qui
nostrum asperiores voluptatum alias?
  </p>
</div>
<div class="div-6">
```

```html
    <span>6</span>
    <p>Iusto excepturi adipisci praesentium
accusantium eius quis!</p>
  </div>
  <div class="div-7">
    <span>7</span>
    <p>
      Lorem, ipsum dolor sit amet consectetur
adipisicing elit. Vero consectetur
      pariatur explicabo culpa itaque qui?
    </p>
  </div>
  <div class="div-8">
    <span>8</span>
    <p>
      Lorem, ipsum dolor sit amet consectetur
adipisicing elit. Vero consectetur
      pariatur explicabo culpa itaque qui
nostrum asperiores voluptatum alias?
    </p>
  </div>
  <div class="div-9">
    <span>9</span>
    <p>
      Lorem, ipsum dolor sit amet consectetur
adipisicing elit. Vero consectetur
```

```
        pariatur explicabo culpa itaque qui
nostrum asperiores voluptatum alias?
        </p>
    </div>
</div>
```

end or flex-end

Items are positioned at the end of the container
`flex-end` **is specific to flex layout, but if you use it with**
grid layout, it will be treated as `end`.

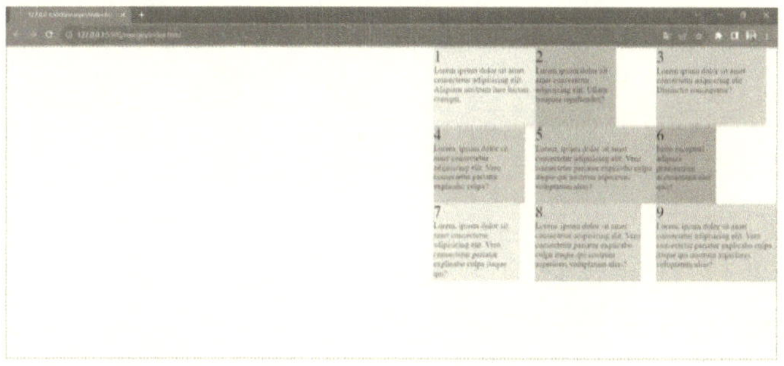

```
.wrapper {
    display: grid;
    grid-template-columns: auto auto auto;
    grid-template-rows: repeat(4, 150px);
    border: 3px dashed orangered;
    justify-content: end;
```

```
    }
```

center

Items are positioned in the center of the container

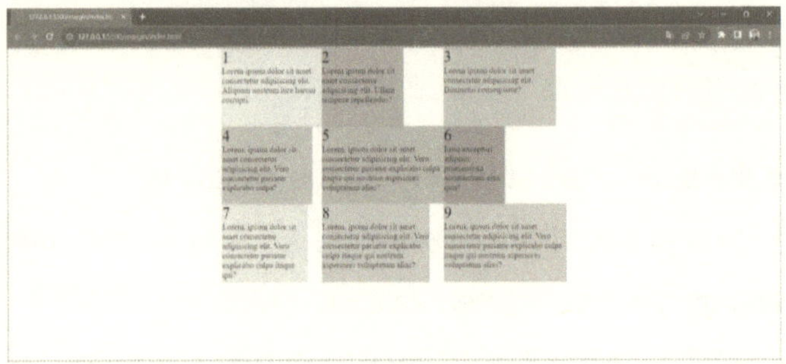

```css
.wrapper {
  display: grid;
  grid-template-columns: auto auto auto;
  grid-template-rows: repeat(4, 150px);
  border: 3px dashed orangered;
  justify-content: center;
}
```

space-between

Items will have space between them

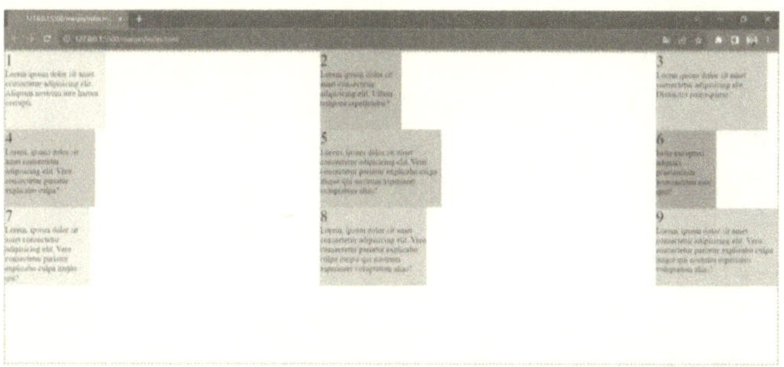

```css
.wrapper {
  display: grid;
  grid-template-columns: auto auto auto;
  grid-template-rows: repeat(4, 150px);
  border: 3px dashed orangered;
  justify-content: space-between;
}
```

space-around

Items will have space before, between, and after them

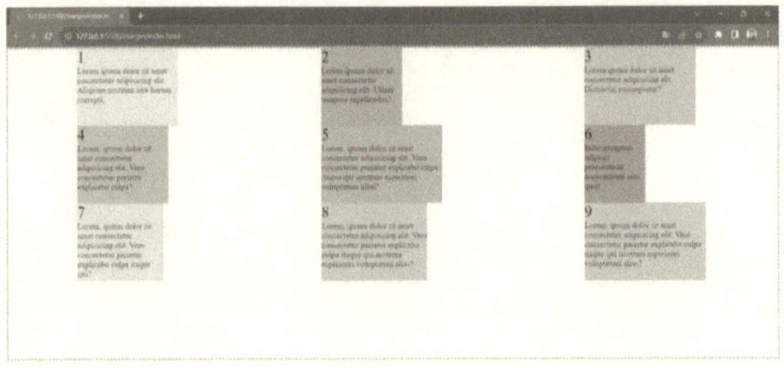

```
.wrapper {
  display: grid;
  grid-template-columns: auto auto auto;
  grid-template-rows: repeat(4, 150px);
  border: 3px dashed orangered;
  justify-content: space-around;
}
```

space-evenly

Items will have equal space around them

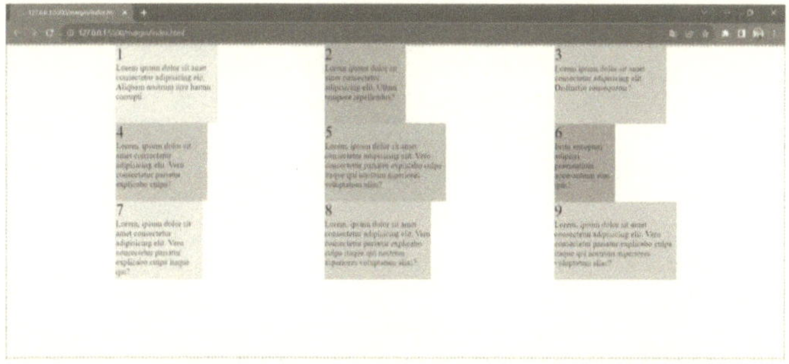

```css
.wrapper {
  display: grid;
  grid-template-columns: auto auto auto;
  grid-template-rows: repeat(4, 150px);
  border: 3px dashed orangered;
  justify-content: space-evenly;
}
```

justify-items

The CSS property justify-items sets the default
alignment for all elements of the box and thus gives
them a default alignment along the corresponding axis.

Values

- normal or stretch
- start

- left
- center
- end
- right
- baseline

normal or stretch

Stretches to fill the grid cell if inline-size (width) is not set.

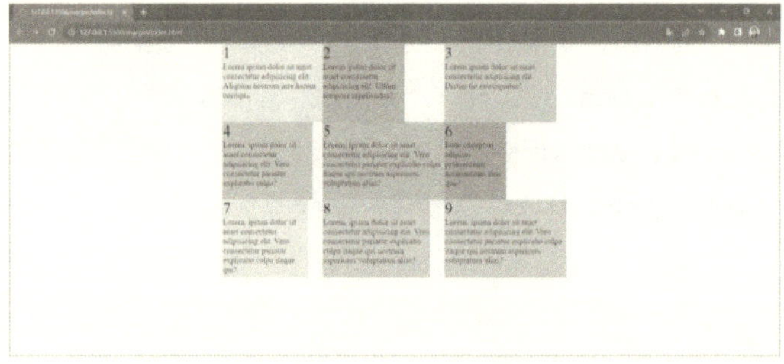

```css
.wrapper {
  display: grid;
  grid-template-columns: auto auto auto;
  grid-template-rows: repeat(4, 150px);
  border: 3px dashed orangered;
  justify-content: center;
  justify-items: normal;
```

```
    }
```

start

Align items at the start in the inline direction

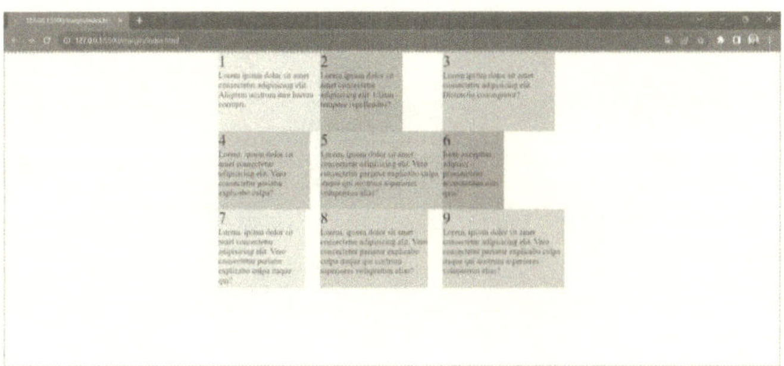

```css
.wrapper {
  display: grid;
  grid-template-columns: auto auto auto;
  grid-template-rows: repeat(4, 150px);
  border: 3px dashed orangered;
  justify-content: center;
  justify-items: start;
}
```

end

Align items to the left

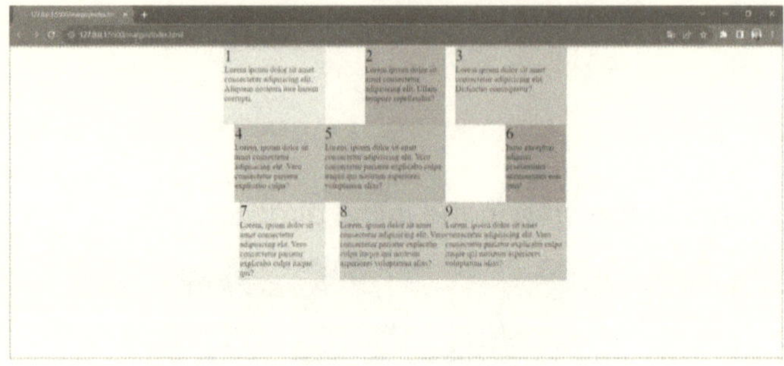

```
.wrapper {
  display: grid;
  grid-template-columns: auto auto auto;
  grid-template-rows: repeat(4, 150px);
  border: 3px dashed orangered;
  justify-content: center;
  justify-items: end;
}
```

center

Align items to the center

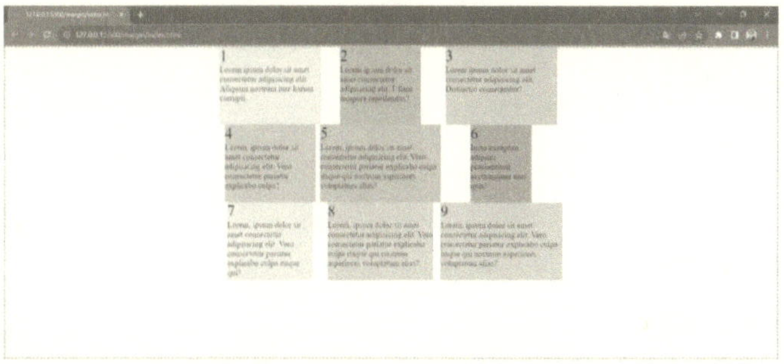

```css
.wrapper {
  display: grid;
  grid-template-columns: auto auto auto;
  grid-template-rows: repeat(4, 150px);
  border: 3px dashed orangered;
  justify-content: center;
  justify-items: center;
}
```

justify-self

The CSS property justify-self defines how an element should be justified. It overrides the justify-items of the container.

justify-self is set per child, not on the grid container.

Values

- normal
- stretch
- start
- left
- center
- end
- right
- baseline

I will give you an example and you can try them all

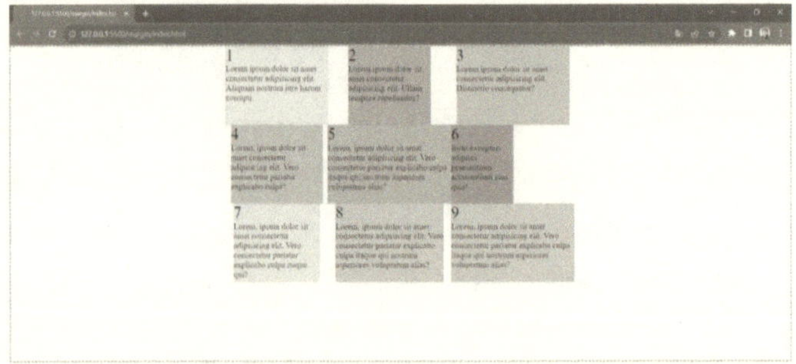

```
.div-6 {

  background-color: mediumorchid;

  width: 120px;

  justify-self: start;

}
```

align-content

The CSS property align-content defines the distribution of the space between and around content elements along the block axis of a grid.

- The `justify-content` and `align-content` properties align **the grid**.
- The `justify-self`, `justify-items`, `align-self` and `align-items` properties, on the other hand, align **the elements of the grid**.

Values

- stretch
- center
- start or flex-start
- end or flex-end
- space-between
- space-around
- space-evenly

I will explain some of the values and you can try them all out.

center

Lines are packed toward the center of the flex container

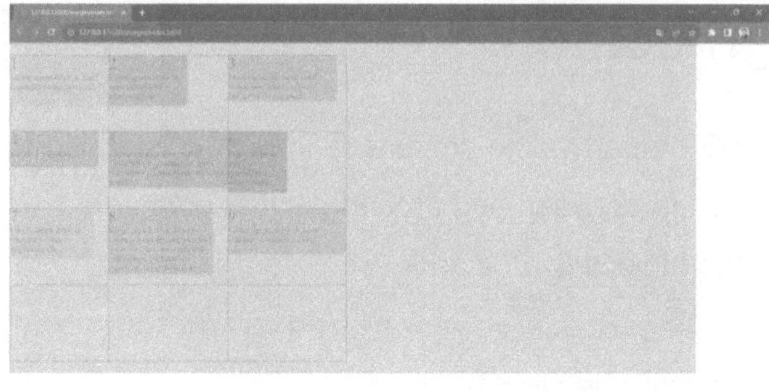

```css
.wrapper {
  display: grid;
  width: 90%;
  height: 90%;
  grid-template-columns: auto auto auto;
  grid-template-rows: repeat(4, 150px);
  border: 3px dashed orangered;
  justify-content: start;
  align-content: center;
}
```

You can see that the grid - delimited by dotted lines - is centered within the grid container. This is the effect of align-content: center;

However, not every item is centered in its row, and we can achieve that with align-items: center;, which we'll see in a moment.

start

The objects are packed together flush at the starting
edge of the alignment container in the transverse axis.

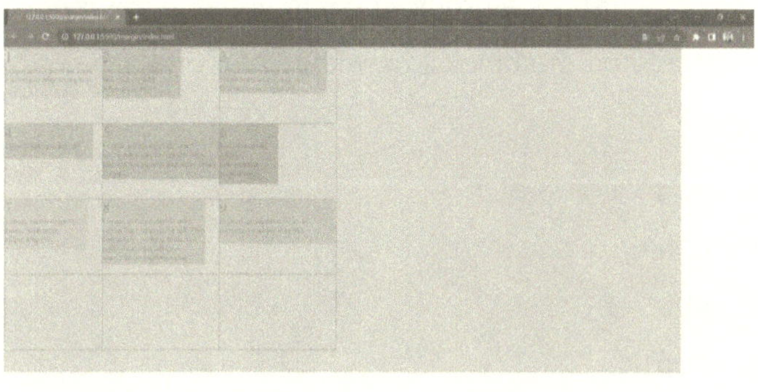

```css
.wrapper {
    display: grid;
    width: 90%;
    height: 90%;
    grid-template-columns: auto auto auto;
    grid-template-rows: repeat(4, 150px);
    border: 3px dashed orangered;
    justify-content: start;
    align-content: start;
}
```

align-items

The CSS property align-items sets the value align-self to all direct children as a group. It controls the alignment of the elements on the block axis within their grid area.

Values

- normal or stretch
- center
- start
- end
- baseline

I will explain some of the values and you can try them all out.

start

Items are positioned at the beginning of their individual grid cells, in the block direction

```css
.wrapper {
    display: grid;
    width: 90%;
    height: 90%;
    grid-template-columns: auto auto auto;
    grid-template-rows: repeat(4, 150px);
    border: 3px dashed orangered;
    justify-content: start;
    align-content: center;
    align-items: start;
}
```

In this example, you can see that the grid elements are aligned at the beginning, while the grid is centered in its container;

end

Items are positioned at the end of the their individual grid cells, in the block direction

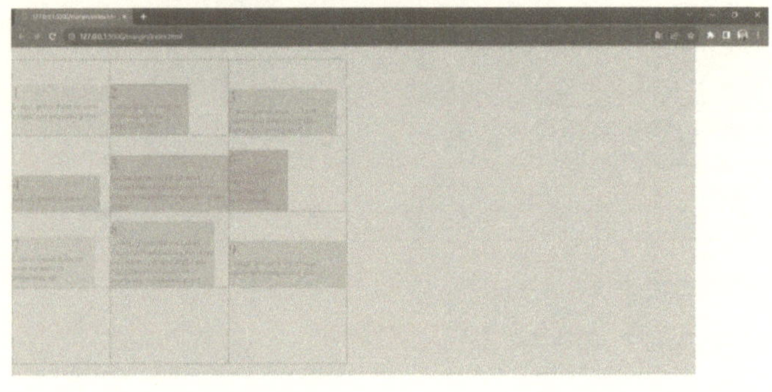

```css
.wrapper {
    display: grid;
    width: 90%;
    height: 90%;
    grid-template-columns: auto auto auto;
    grid-template-rows: repeat(4, 150px);
    border: 3px dashed orangered;
    justify-content: start;
    align-content: center;
    align-items: end;
}
```

center

Items are positioned at the center of the container

```css
.wrapper {
    display: grid;
    width: 90%;
    height: 90%;
    grid-template-columns: auto auto auto;
    grid-template-rows: repeat(4, 150px);
    border: 3px dashed orangered;
    justify-content: start;
    align-content: center;
    align-items: center;
}
```

align-self

The CSS property align-self overrides the value
align-items of the container.

Values

- stretch
- center
- start, flex-start or self-start
- end, flex-end or self-end
- baseline

start

The element is positioned at the beginning of the
container

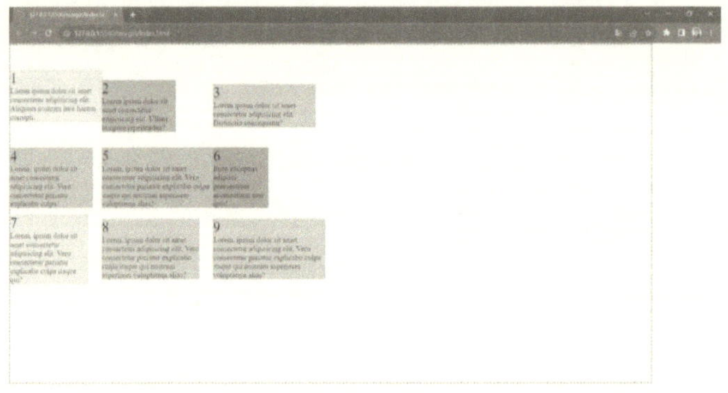

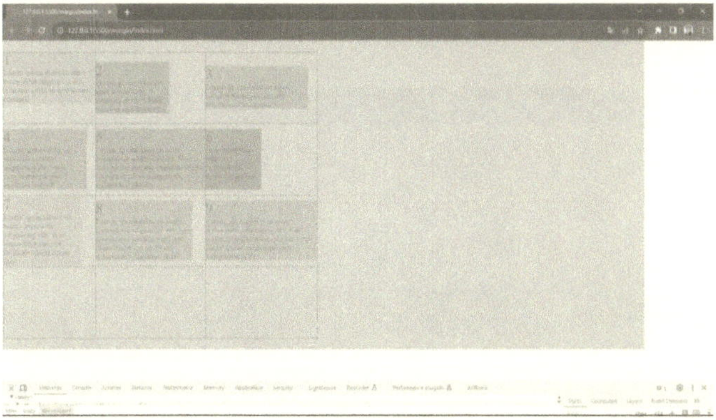

```css
.div-1 {
  background-color: aqua;
  width: 200px;
  align-self: start;
}
```

place-items

The CSS shorthand property "place-items" allows you to align items along the block and inline directions simultaneously. If the second value is not set, the first value is also used.

place-items: <align-items> <justify-items>

Values

- <align-items> <justify-items>

center

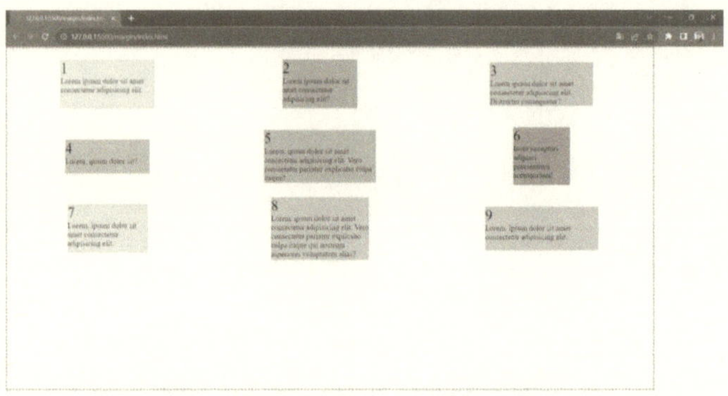

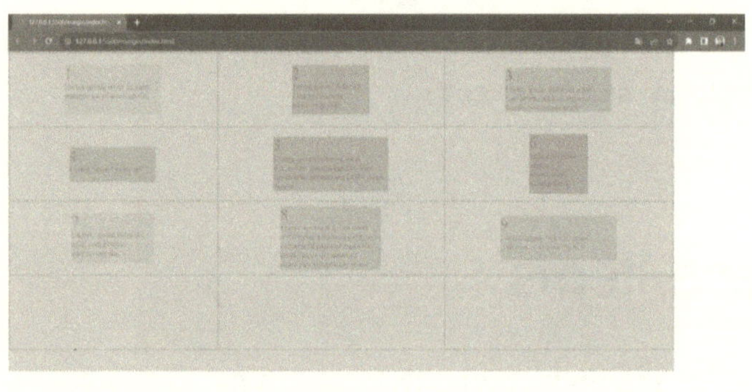

```css
.wrapper {
    display: grid;
    width: 90%;
    height: 90%;
    grid-template-columns: auto auto auto;
    grid-template-rows: repeat(4, 150px);
    border: 3px dashed orangered;
```

```css
    place-items: center;
}
```

center end

Specify the end as the value for the inline axis

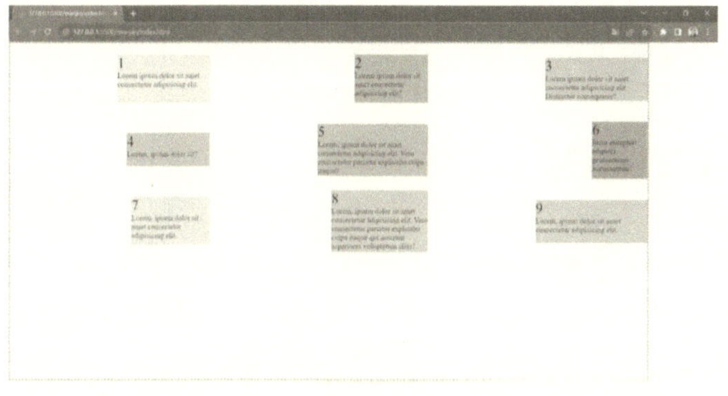

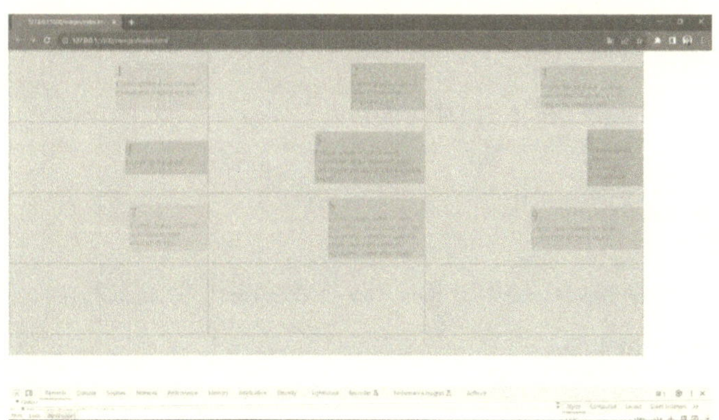

```css
.wrapper {
    display: grid;
```

```css
    width: 90%;
    height: 90%;
    grid-template-columns: auto auto auto;
    grid-template-rows: repeat(4, 150px);
    border: 3px dashed orangered;
    place-items: center end;
}
```

place-self

With the CSS shortcode property place-self, you can align a single item in both the block and inline directions at the same time. If the second value is not available, the first value is also used for it.

place-self: <align-self> <justify-self>

Values

- <align-self> <justify-self>

start center

I will apply place-self to the .div-5 element to place it start center

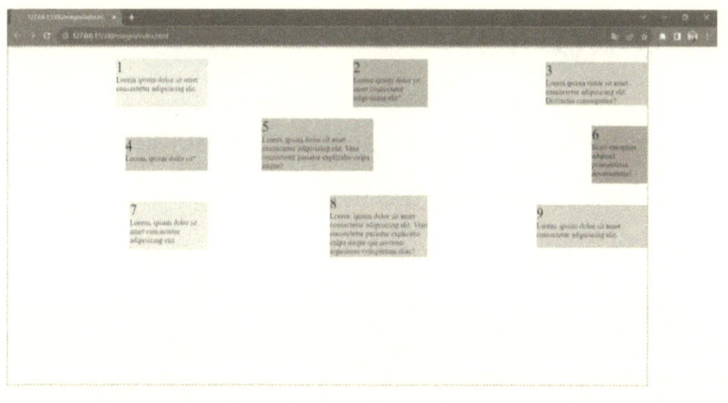

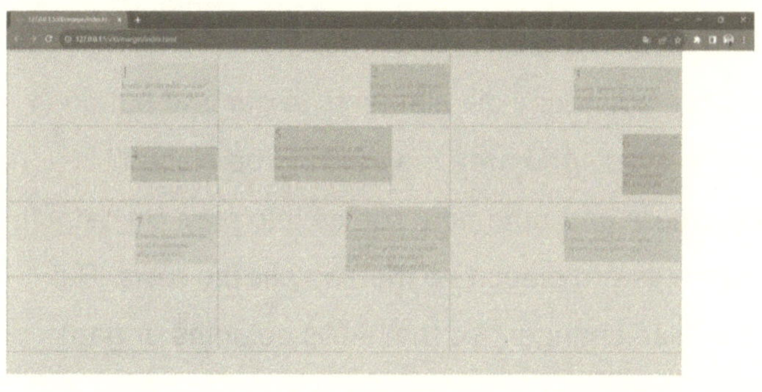

```css
.div-5 {
    background-color: hotpink;
    width: 240px;
    place-self: start center;
}
```

grid-auto-flow

The grid-auto-flow property controls how automatically placed elements are inserted into the grid.

Values

- row
- column
- dense
- row dense
- column dense

What if we add many div elements to our grid but don't specify in which grid area they should be placed?

This is where grid-auto-flow comes into play. By default, the elements are placed so that they fill the rows. But you can also change it so that it fills columns or gaps first.

row

Default value. Places items by filling each row

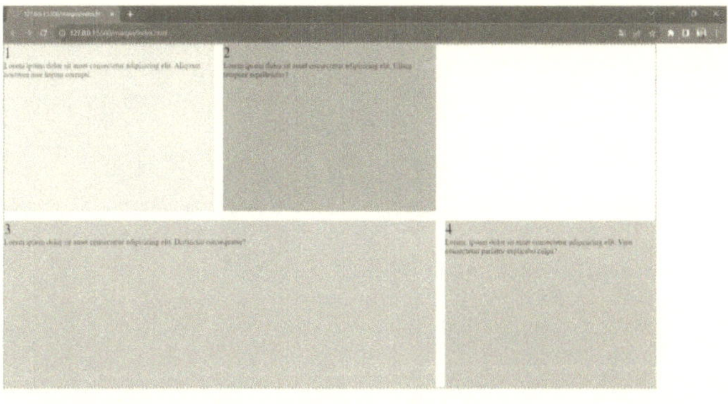

```
<style>
  * {
    margin: 0;
    padding: 0;
  }
  .wrapper {
    display: grid;
    width: 90%;
    height: 90%;
    grid-template-columns: auto auto auto;
    grid-template-rows: auto auto;
    border: 3px dashed orangered;
    gap: 20px;
    grid-auto-flow: row;
  }
  .wrapper div span {
    font-size: 30px;
```

```css
  }
  .div-1 {
    background-color: aqua;
  }
  .div-2 {
    background-color: cornflowerblue;
  }
  .div-3 {
    background-color: limegreen;
    grid-column: auto / span 2;
  }
  .div-4 {
    background-color: darkorange;
  }
</style>
<div class="wrapper">
  <div class="div-1">
    <span>1</span>
    <p>
      Lorem ipsum dolor sit amet consectetur
adipisicing elit. Aliquam nostrum
      iure harum corrupti.
    </p>
  </div>
  <div class="div-2">
    <span>2</span>
```

```
<p>
    Lorem ipsum dolor sit amet consectetur
adipisicing elit. Ullam tempore
    repellendus?
</p>
</div>
<div class="div-3">
    <span>3</span>
    <p>
        Lorem ipsum dolor sit amet consectetur
adipisicing elit. Distinctio
        consequatur?
    </p>
</div>
<div class="div-4">
    <span>4</span>
    <p>
        Lorem, ipsum dolor sit amet consectetur
adipisicing elit. Vero consectetur
        pariatur explicabo culpa?
    </p>
</div>
</div>
```

row dense

If you set grid-auto-flow: row dense, all gaps are filled first as follows

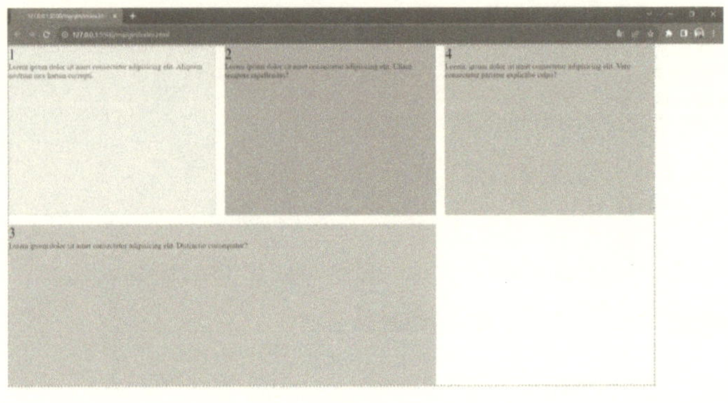

```
.wrapper {
  display: grid;
  width: 90%;
  height: 90%;
  grid-template-columns: auto auto auto;
  grid-template-rows: auto auto;
  border: 3px dashed orangered;
  gap: 20px;
  grid-auto-flow: row dense;
}
```

The same goes for grid-auto-flow: column and grid-auto-flow: column dense;

grid-auto-rows

The grid-auto-rows CSS property specifies the size of an implicitly-created grid row track or pattern of tracks.

Values

- auto
- row
- max-content
- min-content
- length

length

Sets the size of the rows, by using a legal length value. For example, I set 140px for each newly created dynamic row:

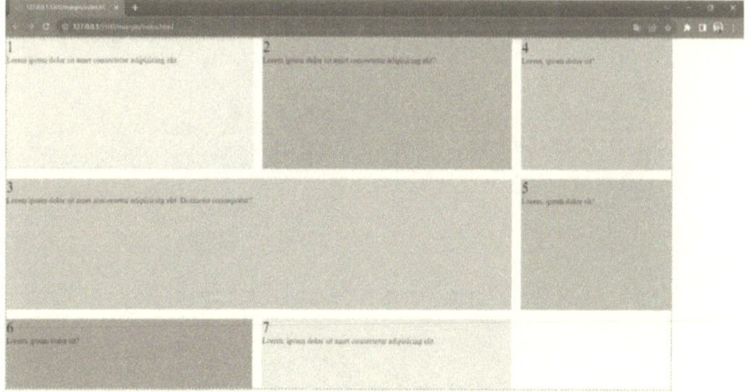

```css
<style>
  * {
    margin: 0;
    padding: 0;
  }
  .wrapper {
    display: grid;
    width: 90%;
    height: 90%;
    grid-template-columns: auto auto auto;
    grid-template-rows: auto auto;
    border: 3px dashed orangered;
    gap: 20px;
    grid-auto-flow: row dense;
    grid-auto-rows: 140px;
  }
  .wrapper div span {
    font-size: 30px;
  }
  .div-1 {
    background-color: aqua;
  }
  .div-2 {
    background-color: cornflowerblue;
  }
  .div-3 {
```

```css
      background-color: limegreen;
      grid-column: auto / span 2;
    }
    .div-4 {
      background-color: darkorange;
    }
    .div-5 {
      background-color: hotpink;
    }
    .div-6 {
      background-color: mediumorchid;
    }
    .div-7 {
      background-color: springgreen;
    }
</style>
<div class="wrapper">
  <div class="div-1">
    <span>1</span>
    <p>
      Lorem ipsum dolor sit amet consectetur
adipisicing elit. Aliquam nostrum
      iure harum corrupti.
    </p>
  </div>
  <div class="div-2">
```

```html
    <span>2</span>
    <p>
      Lorem ipsum dolor sit amet consectetur
adipisicing elit. Ullam tempore
      repellendus?
    </p>
  </div>
  <div class="div-3">
    <span>3</span>
    <p>
      Lorem ipsum dolor sit amet consectetur
adipisicing elit. Distinctio
      consequatur?
    </p>
  </div>
  <div class="div-4">
    <span>4</span>
    <p>
      Lorem, ipsum dolor sit amet consectetur
adipisicing elit. Vero consectetur
      pariatur explicabo culpa?
    </p>
  </div>
  <div class="div-5">
    <span>5</span>
    <p>Lorem, ipsum dolor sit?</p>
```

```html
    </div>
    <div class="div-6">
      <span>6</span>
      <p>Lorem, ipsum dolor sit?</p>
    </div>
    <div class="div-7">
      <span>7</span>
      <p>Lorem, ipsum dolor sit amet consectetur
adipisicing elit.</p>
    </div>
</div>
```

grid-auto-columns

The CSS property grid-auto-columns defines the size of
the implicitly created grid columns.

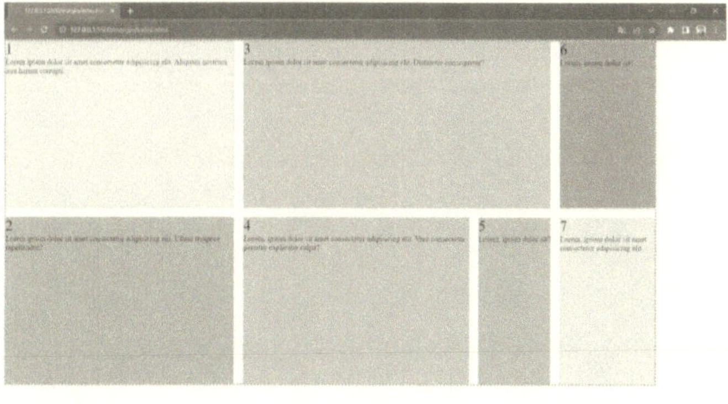

```css
.wrapper {
```

```css
  display: grid;
  width: 90%;
  height: 90%;
  grid-template-columns: auto auto auto;
  grid-template-rows: auto auto;
  border: 3px dashed orangered;
  gap: 20px;
  grid-auto-rows: 140px;
  grid-auto-flow: column dense;
  grid-auto-columns: 200px;
}
```

This concludes our book on the grid layout. Have fun coding!

Conclusion

Congratulations! You have completed the book "CSS Grid Layout". Now you have a comprehensive understanding of the powerful CSS Grid system. Remember that learning is an ongoing process. Practice makes perfect — build your own projects, experiment with the features you learn, and delve into the extensive online resources.

Thank you for joining me in my exploration of CSS Grid layout. I wish you the best of luck on your programming journey. Have fun programming and good luck with your applications!

Media Attributions

Modern annual report magazine page flyer a company
catalog
Image by starline on Freepik

Colorful business card template
Image by freepik

Don't miss out!

Receive an email when Abdelfattah Ragab publishes a new book. It's free and without obligation.

Also by Abdelfattah Ragab

- ◇ CSS Flexbox Layout
- ◇ Angular Reactive Forms

About the Author

Abdelfattah Ragab is a professional software developer
with more than 20 years of experience.
https://abdelfattah-ragab.com

About the Publisher

Abdelfattah Ragab is a highly qualified and experienced software developer with over 20 years of experience in the industry. Specializing in front-end development, Abdelfattah Ragab has a deep understanding of Angular, JavaScript, TypeScript, HTML and CSS. Read more at https://abdelfattah-ragab.com

www.ingramcontent.com/pod-product-compliance
Lightning Source LLC
LaVergne TN
LVHW041731190726
843493LV00007B/2300